D1260473

L-le- lu- ya.

Even If:
The Transforming Power of Perfect Love

Janie Seltzer

Its

Sacred Path Publishing
Carlsbad, CA.

Copyright ©2020 by Janie Seltzer
First Printing, 2020

Sacred Path Publishing
7218 Durango Circle
Carlsbad, CA 92011
www.janieseltzer.com

All rights reserved. This book or any portion thereof may not be reproduced or used in any manner whatsoever without the express written permission from Sacred Path Publishing except for the use of brief quotations in a book review.

——————————————————————————————

Except where noted in the text, all Scripture quotations are taken from the Holy Bible, New Living Translation, copyright ©1996, 2004, 2015 by Tyndale House Foundation. Used by permission of Tyndale House Publishers Inc., Carol Stream, IL 60188. All rights reserved worldwide.

Scripture texts marked NIV are from the HOLY BIBLE, NEW INTERNATIONAL VERSION®. NIV®. Copyright ©1973, 1978, 1984 by International Bible Society. Used by permission of Zondervan. All rights reserved worldwide.

Scripture texts marked ESV are from the Holy Bible, English Standard Version, copyright ©2001 by Crossway Bibles, a publishing ministry of Good News Publishers. Used by permission. All rights reserved.

Scripture texts marked BSB are from The Holy Bible, Berean Study Bible, Copyright ©2016, 2018 by Bible Hub. Used by permission. All rights reserved worldwide.

——————————————————————————————

All design by Janie Seltzer. Public domain artwork: bust of Christ, Rembrandt, Holy Trinity by Andrei Rubley.

Publisher's Cataloging-in-Publication Data
Names: Seltzer, Janie, author.
Title: Even if : the transforming power of perfect love / by Janie Seltzer.
Description: Carlsbad, CA: Sacred Path Publishing, 2020. Identifers: LCCN 2019900878 | ISBN 978-1-7335394-1-8
Subjects: LCSH Poetry, American. | Christian poetry, American. | BISAC POETRY / Subjects & Themes / Inspirational & Religious
Classification: LCC PS3619 .E4682 E8 2019 | DDC 811.54—dc23

ISBN: 978-1-7335394-1-8 (Print)

ISBN: 978-1-7335394-2-5 (eReaders)

LCCN: 2019900878

Printed in the United States of America

With Love and Gratitude
for the SEVEN WOMEN
who mentored me
in the faith -
directly or indirectly -
And have moved up
to Eternity
...passing the Baton!

CONTENTS

"And we are put on
earth a little space,
That we may learn
to bear
the beams of love."
-William Blake

A Love Story

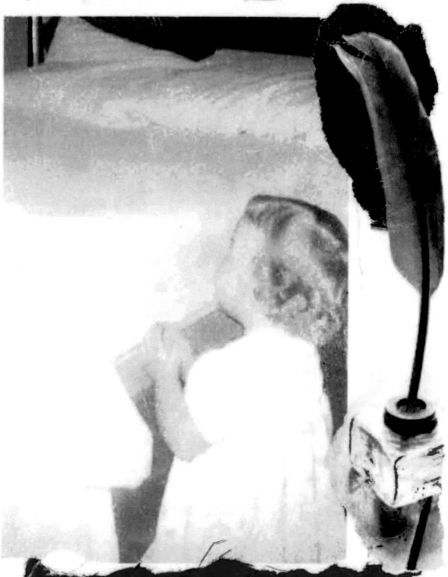

"Truly I tell you, anyone who will not receive the Kingdom of God like a little child will never enter it." — MARK 10:15, N.I.V.

Don't Stop!

You will not be put to shame

This is A love story.
It is falling in love with my Maker—
deeper and deeper.

My journey began a long time
ago — Actually when I was just
A child. I wanted to know who
I was, where I came from.

The questions took me into
More... More than I could Ask
or think.

Take my hand, if you wish,

And ponder my journey. Perhaps you will discover a few nuggets for your soul. Perhaps you will find words, or help for your journey.

My language is poetic and visual because that's how I often receive additional insight for my inner life in Christ Jesus. I receive downloads from above to illuminate Scripture.

"I will never leave you — Deut 31:6, Heb. 13:5 — Or forsake you."

You have everything you need

I will help you!

In short, I receive and see more — about my journey, about God, about me, and about this majestic universe and us — created for the glory of our Creator.

Gift. It's all Gift.

To His glory...

Let Mercy flow!!!

Introduction

It is my desire to connect to the human experience of faith in a creative way. It is how I have best understood myself—and my God—the Master Creator. A student and lover of the Hebrew and Christian Scriptures for many years, I have experienced first-hand that God's revelation also comes through the wonders of nature, and the avenue of creativity.

In my darkest moments, God has sent hope in the form of pot-bellied robins, whippoorwills, and California towhees. In times of prayer and reflection, the Spirit of God has graciously dropped poems unexpectedly into my soul—opening my eyes and ears to mystery, and to wisdom at work in my life—even if I could not see or understand it.

I have tried to follow the Spirit's lead, imperfectly of course, but trusting the greater wisdom and goodness of God—even if the direction was very difficult and even if it brought troubling consequences to others (not my desire, I say humbly). In truth, I have followed the trail of even if's all of my life, though I did not always recognize it at the time. In keeping with the chapters of this book:

—I accepted the gracious invitation to follow Christ when my soul longed to know who I was and where I came from . . . even if I had nothing to give Him but my heart.

—I have received and given forgiveness through Divine collaboration and obedience . . . even if my sins were scarlet or someone hurt me deeply.

—I have experienced miraculous acts and works of God when challenged to believe . . . even if my faith was as small as a grain of mustard seed.

—When directed, He has given me strength to step in for the good of others even if it meant suffering and . . . even if my parents abandoned me.

All of this has opened my soul to more and more of God's perfect, holy, and transforming love. However, it is important to note that the title of this book arose primarily from the poem, "Pandora's Box." Without a doubt, my experience as told in this poem, transformed my soul in astonishing ways. I received profound freedom from the deepest root of human fear—the fear of losing control. It is my hope that by sharing my experience, others may find insight and help for their fears.

"Pandora's Box" is the longest poem in the book and is placed purposely for the end. This first and most profound confrontation with fear actually took place near the beginning of my journey of trust in Christ when I was in my early twenties. The instruction that I received from the Spirit of God took my breath away; yet, the healing that I received enables me, even now, to face life with courage in the midst of continued challenges over many decades of life.

To give context for the poem, I was a student at the University of North Carolina, Chapel Hill, when suddenly I was gripped by a seemingly irrational fear. Completely baffled, and not knowing where else to turn, I got down on my knees beside my bed—with the dorm room locked—and pleaded with God to free me of the fear of having a grand mal epileptic seizure.

Much to my shock, the Holy Spirit of God asked me to face my fear by trusting Christ even if I lost complete control. What? I felt betrayed and helpless. I searched the Scriptures and finally found this verse: "Such love has no fear, because perfect love expels all fear" (1 John 4:18).

When I read these words, I felt even more inadequate, as if I did not love God enough. His simple reply to my soul was that He loved me perfectly! Simply put, I did not believe it.

After battling with the Spirit for awhile, I finally succumbed, closed my eyes, and in my mind's eye "saw" myself out of control, writhing with a full blown seizure. It was unnerving to experience, even with the eyes of my soul. However, within a short time I "saw" the presence of Christ over me—His out-stretched hand over my body—keeping my soul safe even as my body flailed. When I saw this, I knew that I was safe—no matter what happened to my body. At that very moment, the terrifying presence of fear fled.

Over the next few days, whenever the fear returned to haunt me, I simply declared what I now knew: "Even if my body goes out of control, the Lord God still loves me perfectly." I understood in the core of my being how much I was loved, truly loved, eternally loved, and eternally safe. Within a short time, I was completely free of the haunting fear.

There is tremendous relief and freedom in total surrender to God's care. My experience may be unique, but the principle has been helpful to others. The more we are able to release our human pride and our need for control, the more of God's love we can receive.

The more of God's perfect, holy love we receive, the more secure we become within ourselves, or more accurately, our soul—the living, breathing, thinking, feeling part of who we are. In the end, only our holy Father in heaven can keep us safe, as we learn to hide our life with Christ in God (Colossians 3:3).

To be sure, our journey with the Good Shepherd is full of wonder and adventure as well as pain. I often say that if Christ had not prepared His followers for continued troubles in this life, I would have left the path a long time ago! But He did.

And, in the midst of it all, we are constantly becoming and overcoming by His unending grace, power, and mercy. This is the transforming power of perfect love.

There is no question in my mind that collaberation with the Triune God of the universe is what life is all about. Created in His image, He desires to fully restore that image (imago dei) and give each and every one of us meaning and purpose for our lives. The Lord God also invites us to join Him in the pleasure of creativity—with all the various gifts He has given us. We become co-creators with God!

As a final note to my friends and readers, this book is rather "scrappy" and imperfect—on purpose—just like us! We are earthen vessels in the works. It is also handmade on purpose. The language is simple, poetic, and visual to speak to the soul. After all, the soul thinks in images . . .

So, I encourage you:

> . . . to slow down your busy and distracted mind,
>
> . . . to linger in the simple beauties of life,
>
> . . . to nourish your soul and live whole,
>
> . . . to receive the invitations of grace,
>
> . . . to enjoy the Presence of God at all times,
>
> . . . to face your fears with transforming love,
>
> . . . to "Find the Secret of Being Alive"!

This is my hope and prayer for your journey.

With love,

Janie Seltzer

www.janieseltzer.com

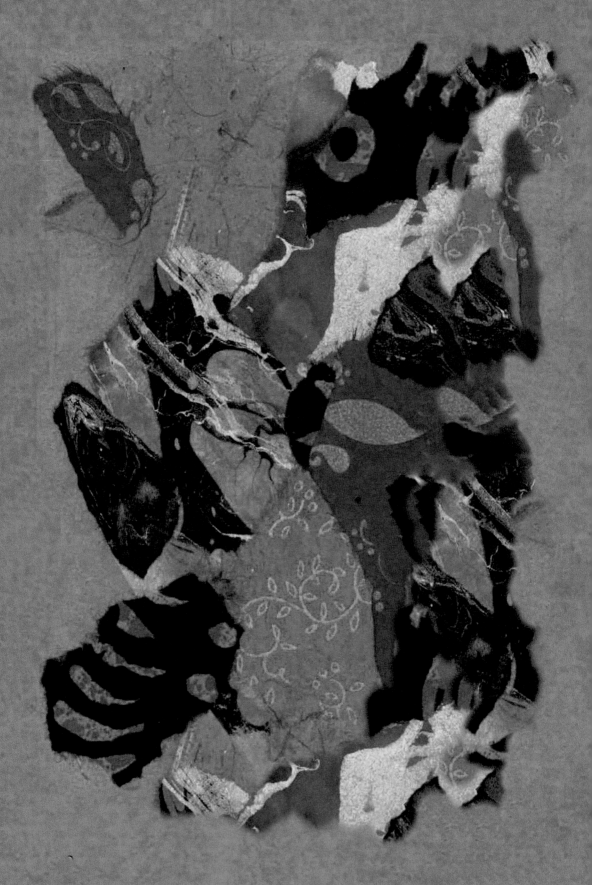

Find the secret of being
Alive
Practice God's presence,
Get into His stride;
Choose a place, private,
Be still in your soul,
Soak in the silence...
In time you'll be whole.

Lift up in earnest
the simple Lord's prayer,
Walk through it slowly,
Instruction is there;
Speak to the Father,
Watch humbly for Jesus;
He promised His presence,
And never to leave us.

"Secret Life"

JTS

17

A Soulful
Invitation

You don't have
a soul.
You ARE A Soul.
You have A body.

Imagine
what one
seed
of Perfect
love can
do!

The Soul thinks in images
It is fed by _Beauty_;
The Soul is the Sum of all that makes us Human,
It is Imago Dei;
The Soul lilts in Mystery...
The Soul is born from Love, is transformed by _Love_ And Returns to
LOVE.

"Imago Dei" ~ Image of God!

At Pritchard Memorial Baptist
When I was twelve or so,
As I rise to sing
A hymn,
Atmosphere splits
With Spirit—
Warm, fluid love
pours,
Shakes my body—
Top of head to toes,
Power sweet
Radiant like fire;
He plants the
Seed of Life
in my soul—
birth from Above
Alters All—
Words, Way, Will;
Little do I know,
He protects my
Tree of Life,
Claim
for Kingdom.

Pew at
Pritchard

You CALL us into the BEAM Away from ball and chain, crumbling hillsides, bribes, and lies ... into Majesty where souls'sit down Around Your feet

where

WHIRLS CEASE; A RIVER of Light— Delights, Heals.

jts

-Wind People-

It's the Wind
Blows you in
From who
knows where?

Let the Wind blow you in!
Beyond Universe... Where
Abba is!
Where Angels bow
before the THRONE...
before the NAME
Above All NAMES— Jesus,
The One who tossed divinity
to the Wind...
For lightness
of Being...

listened to Abba
for us.

jfs

24

—John 3:5-8—

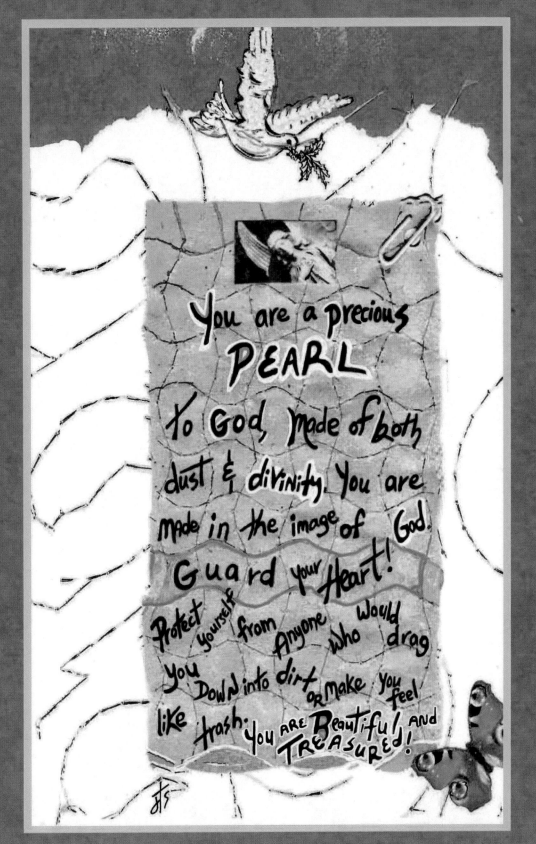

You are a precious **PEARL** to God, made of both dust & divinity. You are made in the image of God. **Guard your Heart!** Protect yourself from Anyone who would drag you Down into dirt or make you feel like trash. YOU ARE Beautiful, AND TREASURED!

"The very hairs on your head are all numbered. Don't be afraid; you are worth more than many sparrows."

—Luke 12:7
N.I.V.

"Seek the Kingdom of God above all else, and live righteously, and He will give you everything you need." —Matthew 6:33

Listen
the voice is small,
still,
Whispers of truth
suited
to the timid
will;

Real
He
comes,

Trust

His
Love,
A Dove
of wonder,
Hovers...
Discover.

jts

-whispers-

Radiant
Invitation!

In the Womb
of Silence
God comes —
Piercing,
Revealing,
Cleansing,
Flooding
With
Fullness.

jts

28

Not fading,
falling
things;
What lives
Forever-
Radiant,
Shimmers
Beyond
All
WE CAN
imagine-
MORE ...
flows
AS A Surging
Sea,
falling Up,
Effervescent
goodness,
GRACE.

dts

"Love is patient and kind; Love does not envy or boast; It is not arrogant or rude. It does not insist on its own way; It is not irritable or resentful. It does not rejoice at wrongdoing, but rejoices with the Truth. Love bears all things, Believes all things, Hopes all things, Endures all things.

Love never ends."

— I Corinthians 13:4-8

Come to the
Good Shepherd...
grace, truth-
Love for you.
Listen to His voice-
gentle, quiet
instruction for you,
Come to the Stream-
cool, tranquil
Refreshment for
you.
Wait for the Wind-
divine, mysterious
Life for you.
Receive from the Cup-
Health, Wholeness
Joy for you!
                    jts

"Come,
Everyone who thirsts
Come to the waters...
Listen diligently to ME
And eat what is good
And delight yourselves
in Rich food. Incline
your ear, and come
to ME; Hear that
your Soul may
LIVE...
I will MAKE AN Everlasting Covenant with you."
—Isaiah 55:1-3 (ESV)

31

Cultivate a quiet mind,
Find the peace
that swallows find;

Widen the range of your
Hearts desire,
Acquire a taste
for Holy things...
Remain.

JTS

Even if you have no money....

- CALLING -

Dare to hear the Awesome CALLING -
quiet, sweet, the silent sound...
Come to Christ your deepest longing -
Heart relationship Profound.

jts

"The wages of sin is death... But the FREE Gift of God is Eternal Life through JESUS CHRIST Lord"
-ROMANS 6:23-

—Maria Boulding

"All your love, your stretching out, your hope, your thirst — God is CREATING in you — so God may fill you. God is inside...

...your Longing."

-INNER Life-

INNER life gives pleasure—
not of this world;
Waters well up from the Beloved
of the Father—
who says:
"May my joy be in you...
HERE Eternity Hides.

jts

—John 4:14, 15:11. (E.S.V.)

– TRANSFIGURED –

Maker of Heaven and Earth,
As I see You face to face
in faith –
And life is Transfigured
by Your Presence,

Fill my Soul with the Wine
of Your Spirit...

Intoxicate me, with Thee –
As I lean into Your Heart,
Marvel at Your beauty,
Flood me with fluid Radiance,
Rejoicing Simply
        in Knowing You.

JTS

"You fill me with joy in Your Presence,
With Eternal Pleasures in Your Right hand."
                    – Psalm 16:11, (Berean)

Something lost,
Something found -
in the ground
around my feet...

where i meet
the Holy One,
who calls ...

the whisper
RUSTLES
AS LEAVES in the Wind,
Longing Rises ...

i turn -
tired of running
UNFREE,

i begin
to Return
All i AM ...

to THEE.

jts

Turn your heart to
Simple things - Alert
to spots of Beauty

Seek the Spectrum
of the light
And go - most of all -
to God,
So Bright, So Bright!

HS

- CONTENTMENT -

-Philippians 4:12-13- "I have learned
the secret of being
content in any and every
situation, whether well fed or
hungry... I can do all this through
Him who gives me strength."
- New Int. Version.

Beauty touches
the Heart
When Jesus comes -
Lifts into Life
What's lost
in deep Night
Quiets Strife
Makes Eyes
Bright

jts

- God Praise -

You give great joy
to my heart; Your life
Astonishes
me within - A true friend,
Closer than the Air
I breathe -
Free to Live and to Be!

- Let Desire Rise! -

It is because I love you, I say,
beware of darkness beyond -
inescapable blackhole,
Apartness.

Let Desire Rise - Respond,
Come to the Beautiful One!

Hear the Sound, Weeping,
teeth grinding - Cut off
from all things good,
Beautiful, Holy.

Let Desire Rise; Respond
Come to the Beautiful One!

Fire furies, Consumes
Stubbornness, Pride -
No place to hide,
Rejection of Radiant Life...

Let Desire Rise; Respond
Come to the Beautiful One!

Gloria.

L-le-lu-ya.

Holiness makes a Way;
Love Calls, points Another Way —
Belovedness.

Let Desire Rise; Respond —
Come to the Beautiful One!

Woe to Rebellion, unbelief;
One and Only Son
Suffered
Made a Way ... Follow the Way
Truth, Life.

He Knows the Way,
He is
the Way;

Let Desire Rise; Respond
Come to the Beautiful One!

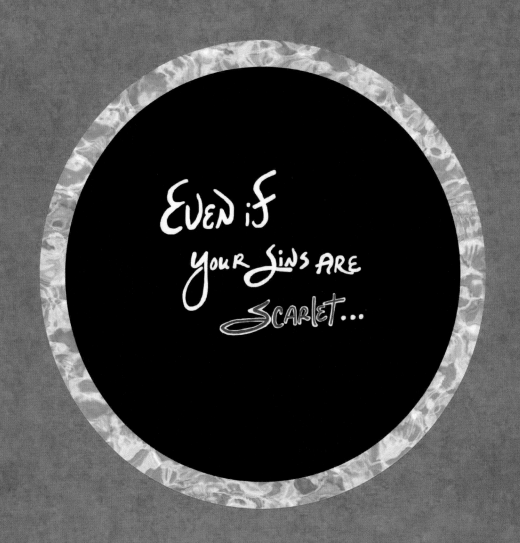

"Even if your sins are like Scarlet, they will be white as Snow."

—Isaiah 1:18

The Crown of Life

Love does
what love must do —
Reduce, Resize, Realign,
Fit for God,

Point towards the pinhole
of eternity;
Wisdom does
what wisdom must do —
Reign, Rest, Resurrect,
A Crown of Life
Forever.

JTS

(The Chaser)

Down, dark alleys
searching shadows–
He comes,
chasing
calling–
Not letting me rest
in my misery,
starting me
in my aloneness.
I stare with cold eyes–
skeptical,
suspicious:
"Go away, like everyone
else — Go away!
I know you find me
repulsive ... Don't
look at me with those
kind, patronizing eyes!
I know how you really
feel, you think I'm pathetic."
"What's that? You think I
don't like myself?
You got that right.
So are you satisfied now?
Go away!
You won't? Ever?

"Sin is crouching at the door,
eager to control you. But you
must subdue it." –Genesis 4:7

48

Please just LEAVE ME ALONE,
LEAVE ME ALONE.
LEAVE ME ALONE...
Hold ME
Hold ME...
Oh, thank you for holding me."

                                    JTS

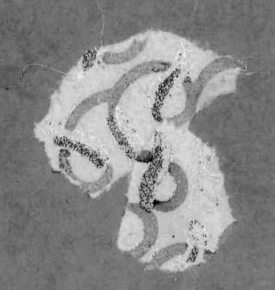

"Come to Me all who are weary and burdened
And I will give you Rest. Take My yoke upon
You. Let Me teach you, because I am humble
And gentle at heart, and you will find
Rest for your souls." - Matthew 11:28-29
                                    N.I.V.

(Blindsided)

Legitimate needs,
soft spots of vulnerability
hidden in the heart —
Enemy of the soul watches

At the most unsuspecting time,
Evil attacks the need,
whispers half-truths,
manipulates desire — traps
by Confusion.

With sudden, screaming need
Lucifer's power prevails —
until true humility
Triumphs;

Purification
of the Sons and daughters
of God.

Holy
Holy Holy
is the Lord God Almighty!

50

jts

(Cleansing)

Holy Father,
Clear the Cobwebs
And Corners of my Soul Where
Darkness Dwells,

Crush the Rush of Sin Within
my Veins ... A World Competes
With eerie enticements,

And enemies Abound!

Shine, Shine the Cleansing
Truth Your Word
Contains, And there
Remain.

dts

"Create in me a
clean Heart, O God"
—Psalm 51:10

"I fear more what is within me than what
comes from without." —Martin Luther

NURTURE

"Do not be Afraid, little flock

For your Father's great happiness

is to Give you the

Kingdom"

—Luke 12:32

Astonishing!   Ask...Seek...Find!

Soul...Live

"What good
is it to gain
the whole world
and lose your
own Soul?"

—Mark 8:36—

Whole

OverComing

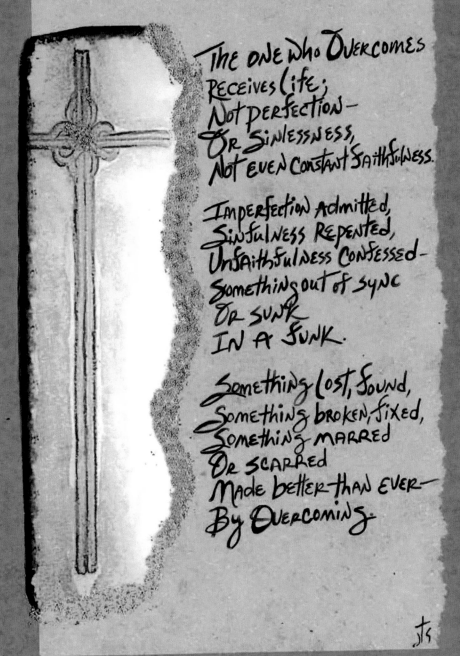

The one who overcomes
receives life;
Not perfection—
Or sinlessness,
Not even constant faithfulness.

Imperfection admitted,
Sinfulness repented,
Unfaithfulness confessed—
Something out of sync
Or sunk
In a funk.

Something lost, found,
Something broken, fixed,
Something marred
Or scarred
Made better than ever—
By OverComing.

JS

"To the one who overcomes, I will grant
to eat of the Tree of Life which is in
the Paradise of God." — Rev. 2:7
N.R.S.B.

-Garden Regrets-

How has the Enemy been so effective
At deceiving?
By enticing the mind into receiving
good with evil.
Eve gazed at the forbidden fruit—
fancied that it was favored, and reasoned,
confused by Serpent's seasoning,
that God would not deprive her
of anything good.

Confronted with a choice,
the honeyed voice persuaded her
to see — this evil as a gift.
Disoriented and intrigued —
With sudden great need—
she seized the bait and ate;
Suddenly a gate of rebellion
rose within her soul.

Truth feigned, the heart stained,
flesh grows pallor; shallow the love
that once glowed bright—
Delight swapped with shame,
fear reigns....
Only the Son remains with power
to crush the soul fiend.

Pow Wow

The flame of human lust
incites, propels, poisons
like a snake;
A taste that mocks
Eternity.

Demons laugh as soul
smothers in the dance
of darkness.

Pray that kind calamity
comes,
Ruins revelry —
Saves soul.

TS

55

Up and Out
Up and Out
that's what this pain is
All about ...
Holy Father cleanses
my bloodline ...
I must feel — even taste,
what is coming
Up and Out —
As fire of God burns
Radiant, poised, Attentive —
Laps up poison
hidden in heart —
darkness only He saw,
Called — Up and Out!

"You spread out our sins before You —
our secret sins — And You see them all."
— Psalm 90:8

Js

Earth and Sky

In the mountains, pine trees
Soar in upward worship,
Rustle from unseen power—
Speaks to my soul,
Connects me to eternity.

But I am here on the ground—
longing for comfort;
longing for you.

You feed me by sun and rain
And heavenly realms,
but I am bound—
Tied to the world—
Susceptible to erosion,
disease, pollution
and beetles in my bark.

Remember to be merciful,
Forgive me for my sins...
And please, Father, give me
A song in the night.

jts

grace to go on...

In this whirling,
noisy world,
I keep my sanity
when I start my day
Here on the ground
with Jesus —
Where He stoops
to doodle in the dirt ...
Waits for the crowd
to come to their senses,
Remember they too are dirty—
Need His grace;
I watch His face
As He looks at her,
loves her,
tells her to go, free,
Leave her life of sin.
That is when the Wind
blows softly in my soul
and I can go on
living in His love.

jts

-Divine-

To be broken
by God,
As a bud breaks
to blossom,
As the ground
breaks
to carry seed,
As a jar breaks
to release perfume,
As the flesh
of Christ breaks
to give life,
Holy, Holy, Holy
brokenness
divine.

59

-GRAND CANYON-

Relentless
Flows the
Spirit of God,
As a mighty
RIVER
cuts through
RED Ribbon,
chisels
CAVERNOUS
CANYONS,

Rushes, Crushes,
Changes —
Forms A NEW
World,
Astonishing
to behold.

jts

Do-mi-nus

EVEN if
you say to this
MOUNTAIN...

Truly I say to you, if you have faith
and do not doubt, you will not only
do what was done to the fig tree,
but EVEN if you say to this mountain,
'Be taken up and cast into the Sea,
it will happen.
And All things you ask in prayer,
believing
you will RECEIVE."

-Matthew 21:21-22
E.S.V.

- 3,000 Miles -

"Behold, I set before you
an open door, He said,
"And no one can shut it." *
Words from Scripture
flash like a neon
billboard suddenly
as I rock
my suckling child;
Spirit sears living
words that leap
from my lap, where
Scripture rests;

Lightning bolts promise:
Miracles ahead
Spirit of God
leads our small family
across the country to California,
charged with new horizons—
God was in a hurry
in San Diego—
people to love,
Shepherd to the Savior.

The Door Flings open !!!
Astonishing miracles
before our eyes
As the faithful hand
of God
Parts the Sea ...
Miraculous indeed
He holds the Key. *jts

* Revelation 3:7

"When you pass through the WATERS, I will be with you;
And when you pass through the RIVERS, they will not sweep
OVER you. When you WALK through the fire,
you will not be burned; the flames will
not set you
Ablaze."

-Isaiah 43:2
N.I.V.

Within...

the tiny
PARAMETERS
of
my
day

Gloria.

L-le- lu- ya.

BLAZE
Lord JESUS!

Nothing is Impossible
for You!

BREAK through ALL the BARRIERS
of your   Holy Will...

...As I AM
WatchFul,
Still.

flow like A
Mighty River
Impossible
to STOP...
I go with you!

65

(Quail Gardens)

Today I stand amid
a forest of bamboo;
The sun streams through,
Cool ocean breezes
Renew my soul.
I listen to quiet forest
sounds — birds on the
Ground, rustle of leaves —
I breathe a prayer that
God would bless our lives
like this Grand Grass,
Not tree or shrub —
Not less or more
than Grass!
You laugh, my Lord
With joy, I see
As I embrace the mystery.

-The Seed-

From a tiny seed, life grows;
No one really knows
the Power
immortal, invisible
Passion of God
in the depths of the soul,
stops spiral down,
poisons deadly pleasure
propels green growth,
Astonishing shoots
of spirit
Suddenly spring up!

JTS

Healing Gifts

Healing gifts flow
down from heaven
when faith forms words,
sees the view
through time and space.

Grace, like a golden
thread, weaves your
heart to His —
flows a river of love,
touches the need;
He is pleased.

Healing Prayer

Joy jumps
in the Soul,
Signals God's pleasure
to move with
Compassion
to Heal

Wait for the Rhythm
of Spirit
to guide you

the Shepherd
of Love
draws NEAR.

jts

69

In Silence
He speaks...
Living, moving
Words
Erase the Bounds
of time and
Space,
Whispers
Grace,
Releases
Space
to Live Beyond Here
and Now...
The Heart Flames
Sustains
for Another
Day.

-Daylight-

jts

Even if
a person sins
against you
seven times...

"Even if a person sins against you seven times a day and each time turns again and asks forgiveness, you must forgive."
—Luke 17:4

"Forgive us our sins as we forgive those who sin against us." —Luke 11:4—

Mr. Grudge is a dark
    Sludge in the Soul —
Hater-Destroyer! Watch Out!
He does Not Shout...He hides
in the Muck... Makes you go Nuts
if you feed him! (Alert, Alert!)
    Starve him out with a Rout!
Bless the one Who hurt you —
    Take her a Coconut Cake,
    Pray for Favor on their Life —
Bury Strife with Love, Light;
    Love makes Grudge
Run from your Soul!
    Jesus makes You Whole —
Win! By Listening to His Word.
                                        JtS

"But to you willing to Listen
I say Love
    Your Enemies! Do
                    good
                    to those
Bless those   who
Who curse   Hate
You, Pray   you
    — Luke 6:27

Like a spider
she spins tales of deceit—
fashions a tangled web
in darkened rooms,
poisons soul
with bitter rancor
of a guilty conscience;
all who enter are in danger.

jts

—Dark Web—

(Bitterness)

Deadly as a Viper
bitterness spreads
unseen in the soul,
spirals, suffocates,
defiles and poisons
the blood with toxic
unforgiveness —
shrewd alliance
to the sly snake
who stains the soul
with blame —
victim again
and again
until life —
swallowed —
comes to an end.

jts

"See to it that no one falls short of the
grace of God and that no bitter root
grows up to cause trouble and
defile many." — Hebrews 12:15, NIV.

A Sword

Pierces soul
When friendship
Shatters — matters
Too dark to discern;
One learns to lean
into deeper wisdom,
Whispers piece by piece
Until the puzzle
Emerges — brings
to your knees
With a plea
for words to heal;
I kneel, know...
Love and forgive.

JS

"There are 'friends' who destroy
Each other, but a real friend
Sticks closer than a brother." —Proverbs
18:24

"THE WORK of RIGHTEOUSNESS is PEACE... Quietness and trust Forever" — Isaiah 32:17 - E.S.V.

TAKE His Hand...
He Will
Help you!

77

THE EGRET

Each jab, stab,
discouraging word
serves to shine
the soul—
As you were
jabbed, stabbed,
knocked down
to the ground,
A crown of thorns—
blood poured round
the Holy Place
where grace
transforms, rises
radiant like
an elegant egret
that soars
in the rising sun

"These trials will show that your faith is genuine. It is being tested as fire tests and purifies gold — though your faith is far more precious than gold." - I Peter 1:7   jts

"God called you to do good, even if it means suffering, just as Christ suffered for you. He is your example, and you must follow in His steps."

-I Peter 2:21

"Even if I am attacked, I will remain confident."
-Psalm 27:3

"God takes a thousand times more pains with us than the Artist with his picture, by more touches of sorrow, And by more colors of circumstances, to bring us into the form which is the Highest and Noblest in His sight, if only we receive His gifts of myrrh And sorrow in the Right spirit."

—Johannes Tauler

Learn to spin your Silk in Secret... where God Unfolds untold Mysteries of your being and Seeing in hallowed Solitude

Joy emerges from Sorrow~ Wisdom Weaves through Pain, and Rare fabrics of faith Flourish in the Recesses of your Soul.

— Matt 6:6 —

jts

82

There is a secret and Sacred path,
A wounded way;

As He calls...
And I follow,
I find

Tender Light,
Restful shade,
intimate talk
For my Soul
to flourish.

The path is worn
and familiar
to Him.

I leanin and get
A closer look
At His Scars.
Now I know what _Love_
must know:

He is acquainted with all my ways
And knows which wounds will heal,

I am stilled and filled;
How I love this holy place.

JS

Raising A Cathedral

When the world collapses
Around you, falling into rubble,
There is a Master Architect
In charge of all this trouble.

He has in mind a Cathedral,
Enlargement of your soul,
Making more room for Majesty
With Holiness the goal.

In order to do some expansion
He needs to tear apart;
No matter the devastation,
Your best interests are in His Heart.

So let God build a Cathedral
that nothing on Earth can destroy;
His ways are mysterious, yet perfect,
In the end you will have great joy...

Watch and see with Astonishment
the Wisdom of His plan;
You will Arise a new Creation,
Held in the Palm of His Hand.

JTS

(COMMUNION)

I found myself in His PRESENCE,
the holy of holies of my soul.
He CAME to ME unexpectedly...
the eyes of my heart saw Him.

His arms moved toward me,
And WE EMBRACED — my Lord And I;
I cried And Spoke Like A child:
"Why did You do that to me?"

"I WAS RUNNING Along so happily with You;
Why did You hurt me so much?
I feel like You put out Your foot —
And made me Stumble, headlong
      on my face,
into darkness within And without —
breaking my heart."

He Spoke Astonishing words:
"I'm Sorry I had to hurt you so much."
That WAS All.
He let me cry in His ARMS.

BECAUSE I love Him more than Life —
I will RECEIVE all that He gives ME,
And Accept all that He withholds...
that is enough to Know.

86

jts

SURRENDER

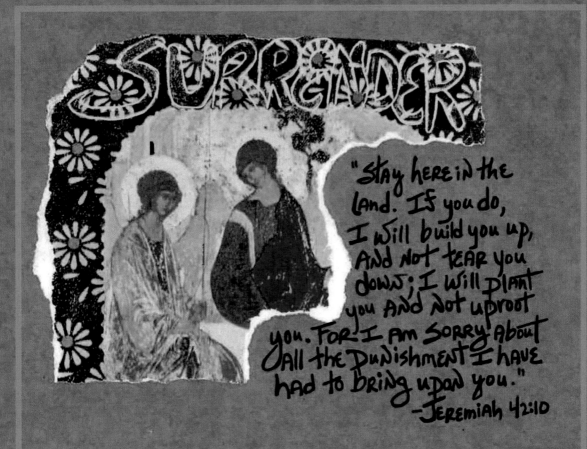

"Stay here in the land. If you do, I will build you up, and not tear you down; I will plant you and not uproot you. For I am sorry about all the punishment I have had to bring upon you."
—Jeremiah 42:10

"For no one is abandoned by the Lord forever. Though He brings grief, He also shows compassion because of the greatness of His unfailing love. For He does not enjoy hurting people or causing them sorrow."
—Lamentations 3:31-33

"For though He wounds, He also bandages, He strikes, but His hands also heal."
—Job 5:18

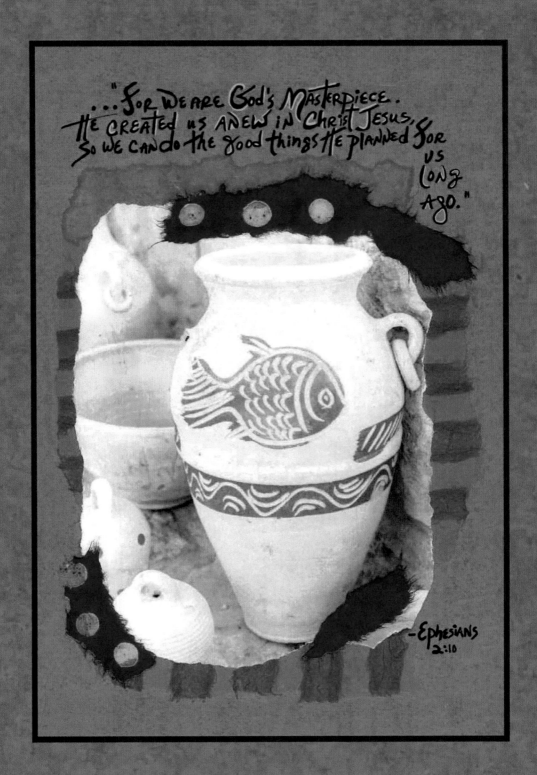

"...For we are God's masterpiece. He created us anew in Christ Jesus, so we can do the good things He planned for us long ago."

-Ephesians 2:10

Dizzy on the Potter's Wheel

I reel under the pressure
of His Hand,

Water splashes over me,
I choke and gasp for air;
He cuts off softened chunks,
Refines the shape
Remolds the inner core;

He whistles softly as He works
I listen to the soothing
sound and slowly learn
Relax... Wait
for the Sovereign
Shape
imaged in
His Mind.

It's
-Clay-

..."Like fragile
clay jars."
-II Cor. 4:7

Grief teaches the Soul
to listen
As dew glistens
on morning grass,
As wind whispers
through leaves,
Trees clap
breathless wonders
of limitless love;
Suddenly
A Robin Reminds —
Plump, Red-bellied, Still
Startles
I AM
Here,
Now.

"The great things of life
Are bestowed upon those
who pray But we learn
to pray best in suffering"
-Peter Wust-

90

(Beyond Blessing)

I bend
bowed by wind,
wait in silence
for you;
My soul waits
in pain;
I remain -
As SEASONS CHANGE...
All green fades
to brown.

I learn
I love you still.
You grow me
beyond blessing.

jts

- Habakkuk 3:17-18 -

"Even though the fig trees have no blossoms,
And there are no grapes on the vines,
Even though the olive crop fails
And the fields lie empty and barren,
Even though the flocks die in the fields,
And the cattle barns are empty,
Yet I will rejoice in the Lord!
I will be joyful in the God of my Salvation."

(CAROLINA BLUE)
I walk down unfamiliar streets
Only a few miles from what
was home. It is March
in North Carolina, and I
like the Earth, watch, wait,
as the season
turns;

Grey, naked tree limbs -
like scarecrows,
Silhouette
Blue Radiance,
savor the hidden sap
of God,
While sparrows chirp
and flit
in Brown, brittle leaves
shed in the onslaught
of Winter;

Suddenly, a whippoorwill
bursts forth a heavenly chorus,
while squirrels gather nuts
for supper;

92

A quiet brook saunters
down an uneven
trail,
Daffodils promise
All is well.

Flowers grow
Outside the
Window
of my Prayers;
The message I hear
Again and Again:
New life Ahead!

Trust Me in the
Darkness, your loss
Will mean gain...

For Each Door
that has Closed,
A Window
Remains!

-Doors and Windows-

JTS

94

A Love Letter in a Black Envelope

I know what you are going through.
I know it is not what you expected or planned for.
From the very beginning, I have walked through this
with you—and I am with you now.
I am your Good Shepherd and I will never leave you
nor abandon you. You are never alone!

I know there are times when you are filled with fear,
but remember—I will guide you and keep you steady.
I know there are things that cause you worry and anxiety,
but I want you to know I promise to provide for you
and meet all your needs.

When things are unclear, I will be your wisdom.
When things are overwhelming, I will be your strength.
When things are stressful, I will be your rest.

I love you completely!
I am the Shepherd of your soul.
I want you to trust Me with your future.
I will do what is good and what is best.
You are safe with Me.

Keep on in My love.

RECEIVED iN PRAYER to
PASTOR DON SEITZER
WHEN A dEAR FRIEND
WAS dying oF CANCER.

A Butterfly!

Home BeCome BeCome BeCome!

- COCOON -

There is Hope in the Struggle, the pain you Endure, God is Refining, making you pure... In the Midst of the Darkness, Confusion and pain, He touches with tenderness, Whispers your Name! Though you feel like a worm in a cold enclosed place - Call on His Spirit to Keep you Safe... Just when you think you might surely die... The Cocoon Breaks open, you Become!

"...And the Lord, who is the Spirit, makes us...more and more like Him as we are Changed into His Glorious Image." II COR. 3:18

"Fear Not, for I have
Redeemed you;
I have called you
by Name, you are Mine -
When you pass through waters,
I will be with you;
And when you pass through Rivers,
they will not overwhelm you.
When you walk through fire,
You will not be burned;
the flame will not consume you.
For I am the Lord, your God,
the Holy One of Israel,
your Savior."

- Isaiah 43:1-3 -
E.S.V.

Loss

Bolts like Lightning
Reverberate,
Penetrate,
Sears Soul,
Push tears to the Surface –
Spirit Screams –
Where is the Comfort
for Loss?

jts

EVEN if
my mother and
my Father
Abandon
me...

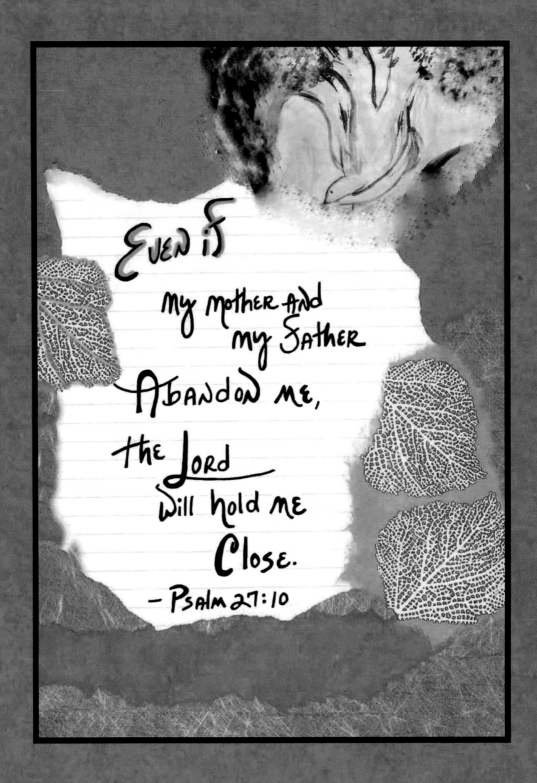

Even if
my mother and
my father
Abandon me,
the Lord
will hold me
Close.
— Psalm 27:10

- GONE -

This time tomorrow
my parents will be gone,
carried thousands of miles
from my heart,
determined to forget
their only daughter —
A little girl who brought
light, love to their lives —
snuffed out.

It feels strange,
the thought —
to have no family ties...
As your family
pressed through the crowd
to persuade you to stop,
saying, you were "out of your mind." *

You said," who are my mother
And brothers but those who hear
the word of God
and do it."
I press in closer to you,
And those who
love you.

* MARK 3: 21-33

Called to Deliver

With a heavy heart
in prayer,
I ask about the burden
I've been asked to bear...

Suddenly, I see myself
in the hallway of a house,
people there... joy, laughter.

Jesus comes, taps me
to see an open door;
asks me to enter.
I see a child in the clutches
of an abuser;
I pick up the child,
walk down a long hallway
to safety.
Silence falls, terror, soul
racks in pain as
family bonds sever.
When I think I might
die from pain, I hear:

"There will always be temptations
to sin, but what sorrow awaits
the person who does the tempting!
It would be better to be thrown
into the sea
with a millstone hung around your neck than to cause one of these little ones to sin."

— LUKE 17:1-2

How could they think
I would drink the
poison of treachery
against the one I loved
like a mother? Why
would I drag his name
into the pit — spit upon
family honor? Father,
forgive them for they
know not what they do!
I shutter to think what
deception will reap —
when darkness
shrouds truth...
Keep me, Lord, or
I will not survive.

jts

-Family Honor-

Daddy, I had a Daddy,
I was the Apple of his eye;
Now I am his Rotten Apple.
He used to call me Puddin',
Now he wouldn't.

Daddy, I had a daddy —
the photo shows his face aglow,
shines with love for his
little girl — squeals with delight
for her homemade cake —
white butter icing,
one simple candle alone
in the middle.

Daddy, I had a daddy,
but now my daddy's gone
without a proper burial
and loving tears to shed.
A thief, stealth and dark —
slipped in with expert subtlety,
whispered lies, twisted
the coils of my daddy's
Heart — No!

Daddy, I had a daddy —
but where did my daddy
go? Who is this man
left in his stead?

JTS

Mother
Please don't turn away from me!
Why do you look at me
like that?

Mother
I am your little girl –
the one you raised...
I have not changed!

Mother
I am your little girl
who stands at the screen door
At Providence Baptist Church.
I cry for you to return
And wonder why you left...
I groan with pain.

Mother
I am your little girl –
why did you leave me?
I am who you taught me to be,
Please don't leave!

Mother
I am your little girl...
how long will it be
before you return?

jts

-Deserted-

I sit in a chair,
Stare at what was
And now is...
Empty Rooms
haunt the house
We shared;

Untimely death
of a family -
Sudden blow-
Who can know
What one day may bring?

I cry in my sleep,
deep sobs
Rack my body,
Wound my soul;

I know they feel desperate...
I still love them so,
Lord, please tell them
I love them still
And always will.

jts

—Heartsick—

My heart—
WEAK, WOUNDED, SORE,
As invisible ARROWS—
Aimed precisely at my heart,
PENETRATE
the core of my life,
love.

Only the living Lord
can tend these wounds;
Only Spirit sees
to heal,
hold me,
love me
back to life.

(COURAGE)

He will bear you up
on Eagle's wings -
Sing a song of Victory
you cannot see.

He will keep you safe -
you will escape
the grip of fear ...
Near ... draw Near.

jts

-Is. 40:31

Shadrach, Meshach, and Abednego Replied, "O Nebuchadnezzar, we do not need to defend ourselves before you. If we are thrown into the blazing furnace, the God whom we serve is able to save us. He will Rescue us from your power, your Majesty. But, Even if He doesn't, We want to make it clear to you, your Majesty, that We will NEVER SERVE Your gods or Worship the Gold statue you have set up."

-Daniel 3:16-18

Even If

Certain of God,
I bow inwardly
to His Will...
Stilled
in gracious uncertainty
of all but Him.
I give myself to His Love,
and choose to believe
Even if...

... All I fear comes,
He loves me still.

jts

III

"Shortly before
DAWN
He went out to them,
walking on the lake...
... They thought
He was a ghost.
They cried out
because they all
saw Him and
were terrified.
Immediately He
spoke to them
and said:"

It is I

(MARK 6:46-50)

"TAKE
Courage!"

"Do Not be Afraid"

LORD of LOVE
Soothe my heart,
Steady the trembling listless swells,
And Rise in the power of your Peace,
Then Fear-Flee!
And I, in Your Presence,
SERENE.

-Heart's Calm-

its

114

this is the story of my own battle with fear . . .

Pandora's Box

This portion of the book, I open my "Pandora's Box" for you to see and hear. Terror engulfed my soul, or so it seemed.

On a beautiful, "Carolina blue" day as a college freshman, I suddenly became afraid of having a grand mal seizure — an "irrational" fear considering that I did not have epilepsy.

However, the fear had lodged in my subconscious when I was a young girl. I watched a T.V. show about a teenager who died on a surfboard from a grand mal seizure.

Just a T.V. show. No big impact... Until this long forgotten image reared its ugly head, darkened my day and my world...

Facing the Fear of Losing Control

A Personal Journey

It was fall when Fear fell...

No one knew
when FEAR
fell -
growl grew
into snarls,
swirls of evil
on an ordinary
day -
glorious really,
bright blue sky,
sunshine,
breezy
bike ride -
Carolina blue
haze of happiness,
Chapel
on a Hill -
young, bright,
Alive in love;

Suddenly
fear erupts,
slides over my tongue,
taste
of terror
tumbles
over soul
in the middle
of lunch,
leash loosens,
hyenas
howl,
hover ...
hem me in —

Cacophony
of pain
Remains...
Threatens safety
Sanity, faith,
All things good
Seem gone.
One day -desperate-
I bow
beside my bed-
lock the door
in the middle
of the day
at Conner Dorm,
Cry out- Help
me, Father!
No one
knows-
but You...
        Help...me.

I open His Book—
Holy Writ
Search words
for breath...

เดินหน

My feet
begin

to Rest
on Rocks
in dark Humus;

Wind
blows
Bones เชีย shake...

I HEAR:

"I Sought the LORD AND HE ANSWERED ME AND Delivered me from ALL my fEARS."

Psalm 34:4

i fall deeper,
quiet...
questions
wind around
my heavy heart;
but...
How?
Then,
I stumble into
POWER:

"Perfect Love

Casts Out

Fear."

I John 4:18
E.S.V.

I SEE, I SEE –
i do not love You
PERFECTLY...

"No" Voice Whispers
in the deep down:
"I love you PERFECTLY."

"I don't believe it!"
Spews out of my
Heart...

He says...
I AM ASKING You to
Believe!

"TRUST ME."

I dive deeper —
"What does that mean?"

"It means EVEN IF
what you most FEAR
comes,
I still love you
Perfectly."

My blood Runs cold as Awe
— billows over... Asks ALL
EVEN if? Even if? Even if? EVEN if?

WORD RUNS WILD
AS WIND blows AGAIN:

"Nothing CAN EVER SEPARATE
US FROM GOD's love.
Neither death nor life,
Neither ANGELS NOR demons,
Neither our FEARS for today
NOR OUR WORRIES About
tomorrow — Not EVEN the
POWERS of hell CAN SEPARATE
US FROM GOD's love."
                    - ROMANS 8:38

I SURRENDER - SINK into trust.

Bird's Eye View...

On my Knees, I see...

A Prayer Vision

i Shake...
Let fear
eat me...
lose control
As limbs Roll...In my Soul
like a thrashing SEA -
furls furious...I see

the PRINCE of PEACE stands by,
extends HAND,
steadies soul,
And I know...
Nothing can separate
the Eternal in me
from His Love...

"The Eternal
God is your
dwelling
Place... and Underneath Are the Everlasting Arms."

Deut. 33:37

The fury flees...

I Rise from my knees whole.

"In this is love: not that we loved God, but He loved us..." —I John 4:10

"The LORD is my Light and my Salvation, so why should I be Afraid?"

— Psalm 27:1

ບໍ ເທ ເປັນ ແລະ ໄທ ອິ ອິ ອິ ອິ
ຊາ ທ່ານ ເປັນ ເປັນ ຖ ອິ ມ ນ ຄ໌
ຊ໌ ອ ຂອບ ສະ ອິ ຊ ນ ມ

"The Lord your God is with you, He is mighty to save. He takes great delight in you; He rejoices over you with singing. He will calm all your fears; He will quiet you with His love."

— Zephaniah 3:17 — compiled

Absorb the Divine...
You will go from Strength to Strength!

"FOR God has Not given us A Spirit of Fear And timidity, but of POWER, LOVE, And A Sound mind."

—II Timothy 1:7 NKJV

"Don't copy the...World, but let God TRANSFORM you..." —ROMANS 12:2

The Atmosphere is different here-

Love banishes Fear, as sweet smells
like Honeycomb fill the Air ...
I am aware of Him -
As birds sing and sun warms limbs,
A gentle breeze blows cool
through branches;
Grace permeates this place
Where Glory dwells...
Angels linger round the Throne,
Eternal Home -
Who could have known?

JS

"Perfect Love Expels All Fear."

-I John 4:18 -

133

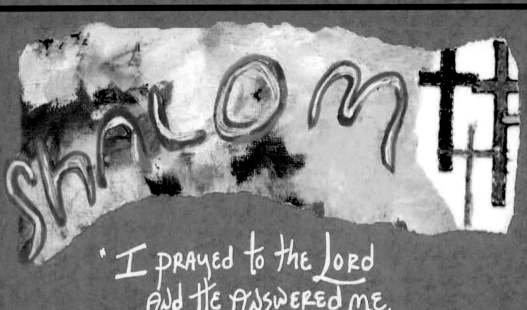

"I prayed to the Lord
and He answered me,
freeing me from all
my fears.
Those who look to Him
for Help will be
Radiant with joy;
No shadow of shame
will darken their faces.
I cried out to the Lord
in my suffering
and He heard me.
He set me free from
all my fears."

-Psalm 34: 4-6

We Will Fly Away*
Free at last from
every ache of unmet
needs, and shattered dreams,

Illusions left, with all that is good —
but not best,
while shadows give way
to the dawning of Day —
shed sorrow for a garment
of praise,

As the soul slips by
a burial ground
of false gods.

Be Still,
Be Still...

The Night passes;
The Father's
Love
Loosens
everything that
keeps us
From Eternity.

jts

*Psalm 90:10

135

- The Man with the Wounds -

There was a girl
Who led a rather charmed life.
She lived in a land of plenty
Where life made sense
And rewards were bountiful,
being who she knew to be;
Smiles won ribbons -
bring her to the top
of the class.

Yet, deep within her heart
She knew, life was more
than what she had...
Wooed by the invisible hand
to a different land -
the inward search began...
for the pearl of great price.

Selling all with joyful vows,
New life began -
As she followed the Man
with the Wounds
and the Radiant Face.

He thrust His finger forward
to a call, the destination
hidden from her sight...

A Master, A Mission, A Marriage,
And life was still sweet,
As she followed the Man
With the Wounds
And the Radiant Face.

Blessings come as years go by —
the vision outward to tangible eye,
But the Man was not satisfied
Until reality took a different turn,
Obscured glory, brought pain —
A severe undoing she never knew;
Trials and testing within and without
Wrap around her soul.

Lost in a land she thought
She knew — dark now the view.
She stumbled in shock to find
bizarre twists in hearts and minds-
Strip her from all she once
held dear — Sears her tortured heart,
A fiery ordeal her only light...
Where is the Man with the Wounds
And the Radiant Face?

He pierces my heart with a sword
And the ache is so great!
I wait...I wait...
I am alone in this place;

Alone to see me for all I am,
Passions, idols and needs —
Locked in human frailty.
I languish in the revelation
of my own depravity —
I share with all mankind,
and wound the Man with the wounds
and the Radiant Face.

Feeling things I never felt before
Wanting things I never wanted before
Needing things I never needed before,
I cry and pray and seek His face —
and find instead a cup with grace ...

A cup of cool water I seize in the dark
and drink to the dregs, and then
find more ... Who brought this gift
I thought I had, and knew not
the thirst? I search for the hand
that holds the cup —
find the Man with the wounds
and the Radiant Face.

He wraps me in a warm embrace,
Safe.
"Hide your life in Me," He says,
then you will be who I meant you to be."

We move past the demon-filled Valley
to pleasant places along the path —
Our destination now clear:
Skull Hill and the Cross.
I am satisfied to discover,
"God gives us the Cross
and the Cross gives us God."
So I follow the Man
with the Wounds
and the Radiant Face.

JTS

Beloved, we are
God's children
now...

When He appears...
We will be Like Him
for we will see
Him as He really
is." – I John 3:2 *e.s.v.*

A FINAL WORD

It is very important to note that Jesus tells us: "Don't be afraid of those who want to kill your body; they cannot touch your soul. Fear only God, who can destroy both soul and body in hell" (Matthew 10:28). These words are riveting and can be confusing because we also know from the Apostle John that "God is love," and that "such love has no fear, because perfect love expels all fear" (1 John 4:8, 18).

So why should we fear perfect love? The simple answer is that God's love is holy. He calls us to this same quality of holiness by aligning our lives to His will (1 Peter 1:16). He also invites us to experience the freedom and joy of knowing that we are loved perfectly . . . even if and even when! The prophet Isaiah explains that if we fear God (reverence, obey), we need not fear anything else! He says:

> "Make the LORD of Heaven's Armies holy in your life.
> He is the One you should fear.
> He is the one who should make you tremble.
> He will keep you safe" (Isaiah 8:13–14).

I have come to understand that the holy love of God gives us complete soul safety—a safety that goes beyond all that is physical and temporal. That is why we are told 80 times in Scripture to "fear not!" In closing, I leave with you, my readers, these powerful, joy-filled words from the Apostle Peter:

> "All praise to God, the Father of our Lord Jesus Christ. It is by His great mercy that we have been born again, because God raised Jesus Christ from the dead . . . So be truly glad. There is wonderful joy ahead, even though you must endure many trials for a little while. These trials will show that your faith is genuine. It is being tested as fire tests and purifies gold—though your faith is far more precious than mere gold. So when your faith remains strong through many trials, it will bring you much praise and glory and honor on the day when Jesus Christ is revealed to the whole world. You love Him even though you have never seen Him. Though you do not see Him now, you trust Him; and you rejoice with a glorious, inexpressible joy. The reward for trusting Him will be the salvation of your souls" (1 Peter 1:3–9).

POEM REFERENCE

About Janie Seltzer, M.A. Pastoral Theology

A lover of all things Organic, Janie is a spiritual director, poet of the spiritual life, speaker, and teacher.

Made in the USA
Middletown, DE
26 September 2020

20388652R00082